How to Do Branding Well

I0466526

Practical Guide

G. Dellis

Effective Branding Guide

1. Introduction

What is Branding?

Branding is a complex and strategic process that involves creating, developing, and managing a brand. It goes beyond just a catchy logo or a memorable slogan; it is a combination of tangible and intangible elements that build the identity of a company or product in the eyes of the public. The term derives from the English word "brand," which originally meant "mark" used to distinguish a producer's goods from those of competitors.

In the modern context, branding extends beyond mere visual recognition. It includes the overall perception consumers have of a company, the values it represents, the emotions it evokes, and the experiences it offers. The key elements of branding include:

- **Brand Name:** The commercial name

that identifies a product or company.

- **Logo:** A graphic symbol that visually represents the brand.

- **Slogan:** A short and memorable phrase that encapsulates the brand's essence.

- **Visual Identity:** The set of colors, typography, graphic styles, and design that characterize the brand.

- **Brand Voice:** The tone and communication style used in the brand's messages.

- **Brand Values:** The principles and beliefs that the brand represents and promotes.

- **Brand Experience:** The overall interaction consumers have with the brand through its products, services, and communications.

Importance of Branding for Companies

Branding is crucial for companies for a variety of reasons, ranging from market differentiation to building customer loyalty. Below are some of the most relevant aspects of the importance of branding for companies:

1. **Differentiation:** In a crowded and competitive market, branding helps a company stand out from its competitors. A strong and recognizable brand allows consumers to identify and prefer a product over others available in the market.

2. **Trust and Credibility:** A well-defined and consistent brand contributes to building trust and credibility among consumers. When customers recognize a brand and associate it with positive experiences, they are more likely to trust its products and services.

3. **Customer Loyalty:** Branding not only attracts new customers but also helps retain existing ones. A brand that creates an emotional connection with its customers generates loyalty, leading to a higher likelihood of repeat purchases.

4. **Added Value:** A strong brand can add value to a company's products or services. Consumers are often willing to pay more for a

brand they perceive as superior or reliable.

5. **Brand Recognition:** A well-developed brand identity makes it easier for consumers to remember and recognize the brand, facilitating purchasing decisions.

6. **Efficiency in Marketing Communications:** With a well-defined brand, marketing activities become more efficient and effective. Marketing messages can be more targeted and consistent, reducing the risk of confusion and improving the impact of promotional campaigns.

7. **Market Expansion:** A strong brand can facilitate entry into new markets or the launch of new products. The reputation of an established brand can open new opportunities and reduce barriers to entry.

8. **Financial Value:** The value of a brand can be directly reflected in a company's financial value. Well-known and well-managed brands often enjoy higher market valuations and can attract investments and partnerships more easily.

Objectives of the Guide

The objective of this guide is to provide a comprehensive understanding of branding and its implications for companies. Specifically, the guide aims to:

1. **Provide a complete overview of the concept of branding:** Explaining what branding is, what its fundamental elements are, and how it differs from other concepts such as marketing and advertising.

2. **Illustrate the importance of branding:** Analyzing how a well-built brand can influence a company's success, improve customer perception, and contribute to business growth.

3. **Present strategies and best practices for branding:** Offering practical tips on how to create, develop, and maintain an effective brand, including storytelling techniques, reputation management, and the use of social media.

4. **Examine successful case studies:**

Analyzing examples of brands that have succeeded in building a strong brand identity, identifying the strategies they adopted and the results achieved.

5. **Provide useful tools and resources:** Suggesting tools, resources, and methodologies that companies can use to improve their branding.

6. **Address branding challenges:** Discussing common challenges companies may face in the branding process and how to overcome them.

By following this guide, readers will acquire the knowledge and skills necessary to develop a solid and lasting brand that can support the long-term growth and success of their company.

Branding: An In-Depth Analysis

Elements of Branding

Branding consists of several key elements, each playing a crucial role in building and managing an effective brand. Let's analyze these elements in detail:

1. **Brand Name:**

The brand name is one of the most recognizable and memorable elements. It should be unique, easy to remember, and capable of evoking the essence of the brand. For example, names like Apple, Google, and Nike have become synonymous with quality, innovation, and performance, respectively.

2. **Logo:**

The logo is a graphic symbol that visually represents the brand. It should be simple, distinctive, and easily recognizable. A good logo communicates the brand's values and creates a lasting impression. Iconic logos include Nike's "swoosh" and Apple's bitten apple.

3. **Slogan:**

The slogan is a short and memorable phrase that captures the essence of the brand. It should be compelling and able to differentiate the brand from the competition. Famous slogans like Nike's "Just Do It" and Apple's "Think Different" have significantly reinforced these brands' identities.

4. **Visual Identity:**

Visual identity includes all the graphic elements that represent the brand, such as colors, typography, layout, and design. A consistent visual identity helps create a unified brand image and facilitate consumer recognition.

5. **Brand Voice:**

Brand voice is the tone and communication style used in the brand's messages. It should be consistent across all communication channels and reflect the brand's personality. For example, a luxury brand might use a sophisticated and formal tone, while a brand aimed at young people might opt for an informal and lively tone.

6. **Brand Values:**

Brand values are the principles and beliefs that the brand represents and promotes. They must be authentic and reflect the company's mission and vision. Brand values help build an emotional connection with consumers and create a community of loyal customers.

7. **Brand Experience:**

The brand experience is the overall interaction consumers have with the brand through its products, services, and communications. A positive and consistent experience reinforces the brand's perception and promotes customer loyalty.

Branding Strategies

To build a strong and lasting brand, companies must adopt effective branding strategies. Here are some of the main branding strategies:

1. **Define Your Brand Identity:**

The first step to building a strong brand is clearly defining your brand identity. This includes defining the brand's mission, vision, and values, as well as creating a consistent visual identity and brand voice.

2. **Create an Engaging Brand Story:**

Storytelling is a powerful tool for branding. Creating an engaging brand story that communicates the brand's mission, values, and personality can help build an emotional connection with consumers.

3. **Develop a Unique Value Proposition (UVP):**

A UVP is what sets a brand apart from the competition. It must be clear, compelling, and able to solve a specific consumer problem. For example, Apple's UVP is innovation and cutting-edge design, while Amazon's is convenience and a wide selection of products.

4. **Maintain Brand Consistency:**

Consistency is key to successful branding. All brand elements, including the name, logo, slogan, visual identity, brand voice, and brand values, must be consistent across all communication channels and consumer interactions.

5. **Build Brand Reputation:**

Brand reputation is the overall perception consumers have of the brand. Building a positive reputation takes time and effort but can be achieved through product and service quality, excellence in customer service, and transparency in communications.

6. **Engage Consumers:**

   Engaging consumers is essential for building a strong brand. Companies can use social media, loyalty programs, events, and interactive marketing campaigns to engage consumers and create a sense of community around the brand.

7. **Monitor and Adapt the Brand:**

   Branding is an ongoing process that requires constant monitoring and adaptation. Companies must monitor consumer perceptions, analyze feedback, and adapt their branding strategy based on market needs and expectations.

Successful Case Studies

Let's analyze some case studies of brands that have succeeded in building a strong brand identity:

1. **Nike:**

Nike is a classic example of successful branding. Its mission "Bring inspiration and innovation to every athlete in the world" is supported by a strong visual identity (the "swoosh"), a memorable slogan ("Just Do It"), and a series of engaging marketing campaigns that celebrate athleticism and personal achievement.

2. **Apple:**

Apple is another example of branding excellence. Its unique value proposition is innovation and cutting-edge design. Brand consistency is maintained through a clean and modern visual identity, a sophisticated brand voice, and a reputation for high quality and reliability.

3. **Starbucks:**

Starbucks has built a strong brand by offering not only quality coffee but also a unique experience. Its mission "To inspire and nurture the human spirit – one person, one cup, and one neighborhood at a time" is reflected in product quality, the welcoming environment of its stores, and its commitment to sustainability and social responsibility.

Useful Tools and Resources

To develop an effective brand, companies can use a variety of tools and resources. Here are some suggestions:

1. **Design Tools:**

   Software such as Adobe Creative Suite, Canva, and Sketch can be used to create logos, visual identities, and marketing materials.

2. **Brand Management Tools:**

   Platforms like Brandfolder and Bynder help manage and distribute brand assets consistently.

3. **Brand Analysis Tools:**

Analytics tools like Google Analytics, Brandwatch, and Mention can be used to monitor brand perceptions and analyze consumer feedback.

4. **Training and Educational Resources:**

Online courses, books, and blogs on branding can provide knowledge and inspiration. Some useful resources include David A. Aaker's book "Building Strong Brands" and the "Brand Management" course on Coursera.

Addressing Branding Challenges

Branding presents several challenges that companies must overcome to succeed. Here are some common challenges and how to overcome them:

1. **Maintaining Consistency:**

Maintaining brand consistency across all communication channels and consumer interactions can be challenging, especially for large companies. Companies can overcome this challenge by creating clear brand guidelines and training staff on the importance of consistency.

2. **Managing Brand Reputation:**

Brand reputation can be influenced by various factors, including consumer feedback, online reviews, and communication crises. Companies must be proactive in monitoring brand reputation and ready to respond quickly to any issues.

3. **Adapting to Market Changes:**

Markets are constantly evolving, and consumer preferences can change rapidly. Companies must be flexible and ready to adapt their branding strategy based on new trends and market needs.

4. **Balancing Authenticity with Innovation:**

   Companies must balance brand authenticity with continuous innovation. Maintaining authenticity means staying true to the brand's mission and values, while innovation requires adaptation and evolution to remain relevant and competitive.

5. **Engaging Consumers:**

   Engaging consumers in a meaningful and authentic way can be challenging. Companies must find creative ways to interact with consumers and create memorable experiences that reinforce the emotional connection with the brand.

Branding is a complex and strategic process that requires constant attention and an integrated approach. A strong brand can offer numerous advantages to companies, from market differentiation to building customer loyalty. By following best practices and adopting an effective branding strategy, companies can create a powerful and lasting brand identity that contributes to long-term success.

2. Branding Process

Branding is a crucial aspect for the long-term success of any company. It involves more than just creating a catchy logo or slogan; it's about building a unique and recognizable identity that can establish an emotional connection and trust with customers. This process, known as branding, includes a series of strategic and creative steps that lead to the creation of a strong and cohesive brand.

Branding is the process through which a company creates a unique identity for its product or service in the minds of consumers. It includes the brand name, design, logo, slogan, marketing messages, and all other visual and verbal elements that help identify and differentiate the brand from the competition. Branding is also associated with the emotions, values, and experiences that a company wants to convey and make its customers feel.

Importance of Branding for Companies

Branding holds strategic importance for companies for several reasons:

1. **Differentiation:** In a competitive market, a strong brand helps distinguish a company's products or services from those of competitors. A clear brand identity allows consumers to easily recognize a product and associate it with certain characteristics and values.

2. **Trust and Loyalty:** A well-built and consistent brand generates trust among consumers. When customers trust a brand, they are more likely to become loyal customers, make repeat purchases, and recommend the brand to others.

3. **Recognition:** A strong brand facilitates product recognition. Elements such as the logo, name, and packaging design help consumers quickly identify the product on store shelves or in advertisements.

4. **Added Value:** A strong brand can justify a premium price. Consumers are often willing to pay more for products they perceive as reliable, high-quality, or representing a social status.

5. **Expansion:** An established brand makes it easier to introduce new products to the market. The trust and loyalty already built with consumers can be transferred to new products, reducing the risks associated with product launches.

6. **Efficient Marketing:** A well-defined brand identity makes marketing communication more effective and consistent. Messages can be more targeted and recognizable, enhancing the effectiveness of promotional campaigns.

Guide Objectives

This guide aims to provide a detailed understanding of the branding process, explaining each phase and offering strategies and best practices that companies can adopt to build a strong and enduring brand. The specific objectives include:

1. **Define the Branding Process:** Examine in detail the different phases of branding, from initial research to the creation of brand identity and its ongoing management.

2. **Illustrate the Importance of Branding:** Delve into how effective branding can positively influence brand perception, customer loyalty, and the commercial success of the company.

3. **Provide Practical Strategies:** Offer tips and techniques for creating a unique and consistent brand identity, developing a compelling value proposition, and effectively communicating with the target audience.

4. **Present Successful Case Studies:**
Analyze examples of brands that have
successfully implemented branding strategies,
identifying the keys to their success and the
lessons learned.

5. **Explore Branding Challenges:** Discuss
the main difficulties that companies may
encounter in the branding process and how to
address them to maintain a strong and
consistent brand over time.

The Branding Process: A Detailed
Analysis

1. Research and Analysis

The branding process begins with a phase of
research and analysis, essential for
understanding the market, target audience, and

competition. This phase allows the collection of valuable information that will guide strategic decisions in the branding process.

1.1 Market Analysis:

Market analysis involves evaluating current trends, opportunities, and threats in the sector in which the company operates. This includes analyzing market size, growth rate, entry barriers, and emerging technologies.

1.2 Target Audience Analysis:

Understanding the target audience is essential for creating a brand that resonates with consumers. Demographic, psychographic, and behavioral analysis of the audience helps identify consumers' needs, desires, purchasing habits, and pain points. Tools such as surveys, focus groups, and customer data analysis can be used to gather this information.

1.3 Competitor Analysis:

Competitor analysis helps identify the

strengths and weaknesses of competitors, as well as opportunities for differentiation. This includes evaluating competing brands, their marketing strategies, products and services offered, and consumer perceptions.

2. Defining Brand Identity

Once the research and analysis phase is complete, the next step is to define the brand identity. This phase includes defining the brand's mission, vision, values, personality, and unique value proposition.

2.1 Mission and Vision:

The brand's mission describes the primary purpose of the company and what it aims to achieve. The vision, on the other hand, represents the company's long-term goal and future aspirations. Well-defined mission and vision help guide strategic decisions and communicate the brand's direction to customers and employees.

2.2 Brand Values:

Brand values are the fundamental principles that guide the company and define its culture and behavior. They represent what the company believes in and influence the perception of the brand by consumers.

2.3 Brand Personality:

Brand personality is how the brand is perceived by consumers. It can be described as a set of human traits attributed to the brand, such as being friendly, reliable, innovative, or luxurious. Brand personality helps create an emotional connection with consumers and differentiate from the competition.

2.4 Unique Value Proposition (UVP):

The UVP is what distinguishes the brand from its competitors. It must be clear, compelling, and able to solve a specific consumer problem. The UVP communicates the unique value that the brand offers and why consumers should choose the brand over others.

3. Creating Visual and Verbal Brand Elements

With the brand identity well-defined, the next step is to create the visual and verbal elements that will represent the brand. This includes the brand name, logo, slogan, colors, typefaces, and other graphic elements.

3.1 Brand Name:

The brand name must be unique, easy to remember, and able to evoke the essence of the brand. It must also be easy to pronounce and write and be registrable as a trademark.

3.2 Logo:

The logo is a graphic symbol that visually represents the brand. It must be simple, distinctive, and easily recognizable. A good logo communicates the brand's values and creates a lasting impression.

3.3 Slogan:

The slogan is a short and memorable phrase that captures the essence of the brand. It must be compelling and able to differentiate the brand from the competition. An effective slogan communicates the unique value of the brand clearly and concisely.

3.4 Visual Identity:

The visual identity includes all the graphic elements that represent the brand, including colors, typefaces, layouts, and designs. A consistent visual identity helps create a unified brand image and facilitates consumer recognition.

4. Developing the Communication Strategy

The brand communication strategy is essential

for spreading the brand message and reaching the target audience. This phase includes defining communication channels, key messages, and marketing campaigns.

4.1 Communication Channels:

The choice of communication channels depends on the target audience and marketing objectives. Channels can include traditional media (TV, radio, print), digital media (websites, social media, email marketing), and direct touchpoints (events, physical stores).

4.2 Key Messages:

Key messages must be consistent with the brand identity and clearly communicate the unique value proposition. They must be adapted to different communication channels and the target audience, while maintaining overall consistency.

4.3 Marketing Campaigns:

Marketing campaigns must be creative and

engaging, promoting the brand's values and unique value proposition. Campaigns can include advertising, promotions, PR, content marketing, and other promotional activities.

5. Brand Implementation and Management

Once the branding strategy is developed, it's time to implement and continuously manage it. This phase includes staff training, performance monitoring, and strategy adjustments based on feedback and analysis.

5.1 Staff Training:

Staff must be trained on the brand identity and its importance. All employees must understand the brand values and know how to communicate and represent the brand consistently.

5.2 Performance Monitoring:

Monitoring brand performance is essential to evaluate the effectiveness of branding strategies. This includes analyzing marketing metrics, customer feedback, and brand perceptions.

5.3 Strategy Adaptation:

Branding is an ongoing process that requires constant adjustments. Companies must be ready to modify their strategies based on market changes, new trends, and consumer feedback.

6. Measuring Brand Success

Measuring brand success is essential to understand if the adopted strategies are working and to identify areas for improvement. This can be done through a series of metrics and key performance indicators (KPIs).

6.1 Brand Awareness:

Brand awareness measures how well consumers know and recognize the brand. This can be assessed through surveys, market research, and social media data analysis.

6.2 Brand Perception:

Brand perception evaluates how consumers view the brand in terms of values, personality, and reputation. This can be measured through customer satisfaction surveys and online review analysis.

6.3 Customer Loyalty:

Customer loyalty measures the propensity of consumers to make repeat purchases and recommend the brand to others. This can be assessed through customer retention metrics and loyalty programs.

6.4 Financial Performance:

The financial performance of the brand can be measured through indicators such as revenue, profit margin, and market share. A strong brand should positively contribute to the company's financial performance.

6.5 Social Media Engagement:

Social media engagement measures how much consumers interact with the brand online. This can be assessed through metrics such as the number of likes, comments, shares, and followers on social media.

Branding Strategies and Best Practices

Defining a Clear Vision

A clear and well-defined vision is fundamental for branding success. The vision must be ambitious yet realistic, and it should inspire and guide all company activities. Here are some tips for defining a clear vision:

1. **Involve the Leadership Team:** The vision definition should involve the company's leadership team, which must be aligned and committed to pursuing the vision.

2. **Communicate the Vision:** The vision must be communicated clearly and consistently to all company stakeholders, including employees, customers, and partners.

3. **Make the Vision Tangible:** The vision must be translated into concrete objectives and measurable actions, to ensure that it becomes a reality and is not just a statement on paper.

Building a Strong Brand Identity

Building a strong brand identity requires

consistency, creativity, and attention to detail. Here are some strategies for creating a compelling brand identity:

1. **Be Authentic:** The brand identity must be authentic and reflect the company's true values and personality. Consumers can recognize insincerity, and an inauthentic brand risks losing credibility.

2. **Create an Emotional Connection:** A strong brand identity creates an emotional connection with consumers. This can be achieved through storytelling, sharing brand history, and creating experiences that resonate with consumers on an emotional level.

3. **Ensure Consistency:** Brand identity must be consistent across all touchpoints and communication channels. This includes visual elements, tone of voice, and key messages.

Engaging with the Target Audience

Effective branding requires a deep understanding of the target audience and a proactive engagement strategy. Here are some tips for engaging with the target audience:

1. **Listen to Your Customers:** Understanding consumer needs and desires is essential for creating a brand that resonates. Companies should actively listen to their customers through surveys, social media, and direct feedback.

2. **Create Valuable Content:** Providing valuable content that meets the needs of the target audience is an effective way to engage and build trust. This can include blog posts, videos, guides, and interactive content.

3. **Be Present on Social Media:** Social media is a powerful tool for engaging with the target audience. Companies must be present on the social platforms most frequented by their target audience and engage with them

through posts, comments, and messages.

Measuring and Adjusting Branding Strategies

Measuring the effectiveness of branding strategies is crucial for making informed decisions and adjustments. Here are some tips for measuring and adjusting branding strategies:

1. **Set Clear Objectives:** Branding objectives must be clear and measurable. This includes defining specific KPIs to evaluate performance.

2. **Analyze Data:** Data analysis is essential for understanding the effectiveness of branding strategies. This can include analyzing marketing metrics, consumer feedback, and sales data.

3. **Be Ready to Adapt:** Branding is an ongoing process that requires constant adjustments. Companies must be ready to modify their strategies based on analysis and market changes.

Successful Branding Case Studies

Case Study 1: Apple

Overview:

Apple is a global leader in technology and one of the most valuable brands in the world. The company has built a strong brand identity based on innovation, design, and user experience.

Branding Strategies:

1. **Consistent Visual Identity:** Apple's

visual identity is clean, minimalist, and instantly recognizable. The iconic logo and sleek product design are central to the brand's appeal.

2. **Strong Brand Values:** Apple's brand values include innovation, quality, and simplicity. These values are consistently communicated through all brand touchpoints.

3. **Emotional Connection:** Apple has created an emotional connection with consumers by focusing on user experience and creating products that inspire and empower users.

Results:

Apple's branding strategies have led to strong brand loyalty, high customer satisfaction, and a leading position in the technology market. The company's brand is a significant contributor to its financial success and market leadership.

Case Study 2: Nike

Overview:

Nike is a leading brand in the sportswear and athletic footwear industry. The company has built a strong brand identity based on performance, innovation, and inspiration.

Branding Strategies:

1. **Powerful Slogan:** Nike's "Just Do It" slogan is one of the most recognizable in the world and effectively communicates the brand's values of determination and perseverance.

2. **Emotional Storytelling:** Nike uses storytelling to create an emotional connection with consumers. Marketing campaigns often feature athletes and stories of overcoming challenges.

3. **Consistent Brand Experience:** Nike ensures a consistent brand experience across all touchpoints, including product design, retail stores, and online presence.

Results:

Nike's branding strategies have resulted in high brand awareness, strong customer loyalty, and a leading position in the sportswear market. The brand's ability to inspire and connect with consumers has been key to its success.

Case Study 3: Coca-Cola

Overview:

Coca-Cola is one of the most iconic and recognizable brands in the world. The company has built a strong brand identity based on happiness, sharing, and tradition.

Branding Strategies:

1. **Iconic Visual Identity:** Coca-Cola's red and white color scheme and distinctive logo are instantly recognizable. The brand's visual identity has remained consistent over the years.

2. **Emotional Marketing:** Coca-Cola's marketing campaigns focus on creating emotional connections with consumers. Campaigns often feature themes of happiness, friendship, and celebration.

3. **Global Consistency:** Coca-Cola ensures brand consistency on a global scale, adapting marketing messages to different cultures while maintaining the core brand values.

Results:

Coca-Cola's branding strategies have resulted in strong brand recognition, high consumer loyalty, and a leading position in the beverage market. The brand's ability to evoke positive emotions has been key to its enduring success.

Challenges in Branding

Despite the potential benefits, the branding process is not without its challenges. Companies may face various obstacles that can hinder the development and management of a strong brand.

1. Maintaining Consistency

Maintaining brand consistency across all touchpoints and channels is a significant challenge. Inconsistencies in visual elements, messaging, and customer experience can confuse consumers and weaken the brand.

Strategies to Overcome:

1. **Develop Brand Guidelines:** Create comprehensive brand guidelines that detail how the brand should be represented visually and verbally across all channels.

2. **Train Employees:** Ensure that all employees understand and adhere to the brand guidelines. Provide training and resources to help them represent the brand consistently.

2. Adapting to Market Changes

The market environment is constantly evolving, and companies must adapt their branding strategies to stay relevant. Changes in consumer preferences, technological advancements, and competitive pressures can impact the effectiveness of branding strategies.

Strategies to Overcome:

1. **Stay Informed:** Continuously monitor market trends, consumer behavior, and competitive activities to identify changes and opportunities.

2. **Be Agile:** Develop flexible branding strategies that can be quickly adapted to respond to market changes. This may include updating brand messages, refreshing visual elements, or launching new products.

3. Protecting Brand Reputation

Protecting the brand reputation is crucial for maintaining consumer trust and loyalty. Negative publicity, product recalls, and social media controversies can damage the brand and erode consumer confidence.

Strategies to Overcome:

1. **Proactive PR:** Develop a proactive public relations strategy to manage and protect the brand reputation. This includes monitoring media coverage, engaging with consumers, and addressing issues promptly.

2. **Crisis Management:** Prepare a crisis management plan to handle potential brand crises. This plan should outline the steps to be taken in the event of a crisis, including communication strategies and corrective actions.

Conclusion

Branding is a complex and ongoing process that requires strategic planning, creativity, and continuous management. A strong brand can differentiate a company from its competitors, build trust and loyalty among consumers, and drive long-term commercial success. By following the steps outlined in this guide and adopting best practices, companies can create and maintain a powerful brand that resonates with consumers and achieves lasting success.

3.Market Analysis and Target Audience Definition in Branding

Branding is a fundamental process for any company aiming to stand out in a competitive market. A key element of branding is a thorough understanding of the market and a clear definition of the target audience. These steps are crucial for creating a brand that resonates with the desired audience and can sustain a long-term competitive advantage. This document explores in detail market analysis and target audience definition in the context of branding, providing a comprehensive guide on how to effectively execute these processes.

Market Analysis

Market analysis is the process of gathering, analyzing, and interpreting data related to the market in which a company operates or intends to operate. This process is essential for understanding market dynamics, identifying opportunities and threats, and informing strategic decisions.

1. Objectives of Market Analysis

The main objectives of market analysis include:

- **Understanding the market:** Identifying market size, market segments, trends, and dynamics.

- **Evaluating competition:** Analyzing major competitors, their strengths and weaknesses, strategies, and performance.

- **Identifying the target audience:** Determining who potential customers are and their needs, preferences, and behaviors.

- **Identifying opportunities and threats:** Recognizing market opportunities and threats that could affect the company.

2. Stages of Market Analysis

Market analysis consists of several stages, each crucial for gathering and interpreting necessary information.

2.1 Information Gathering

Information gathering is the first step in market analysis and can be divided into two main categories: primary data and secondary data.

- **Primary data:** These are data collected directly from the market through methods such as surveys, interviews, focus groups, and direct observation. Primary data are specific and relevant to the company collecting them.

- **Secondary data:** These are pre-existing data collected from sources like market reports, industry publications, government statistics, and academic studies. Secondary data are useful for obtaining a general overview of the market and trends.

2.2 Data Analysis

After gathering information, the next step is data analysis to extract useful insights. This process includes:

- **Market segmentation:** Dividing the market into distinct segments based on demographic, psychographic, geographic, and behavioral characteristics.

- **SWOT analysis:** Assessing the strengths, weaknesses, opportunities, and threats of the market to identify areas of competitive advantage and risk.

- **Competitive analysis:** Examining major competitors to understand their strategies, strengths, weaknesses, and market positions.

2.3 Interpretation of Results

Interpreting the results of data analysis allows drawing meaningful conclusions and making strategic recommendations. This includes:

- **Identifying market opportunities:** Recognizing potential growth areas and untapped market niches.

- **Evaluating threats:** Understanding challenges the company might face and developing strategies to mitigate risks.

- **Defining market positioning:** Determining how the brand can differentiate itself from competitors and what unique value it can offer to consumers.

Target Audience Definition

Defining the target audience is one of the most critical steps in the branding process. A well-defined target allows focusing marketing strategies, improving communication effectiveness, and increasing the likelihood of brand success.

1. Importance of Target Definition

Clearly defining the target audience is essential for several reasons:

- **Customization of marketing strategies:** Allows creating targeted messages and advertising campaigns that resonate with a specific audience.

- **Resource efficiency:** Focusing marketing efforts and resources on a specific consumer segment reduces waste and increases effectiveness.

- **Better understanding of customers:** Helps in better understanding customer needs, desires, and behaviors, improving the ability to satisfy them.

2. Market Segmentation

Market segmentation is the process of dividing the market into distinct groups of consumers who share similar characteristics. This helps to identify the target audience more precisely. There are several bases for market segmentation:

2.1 Demographic Segmentation

Demographic segmentation divides the market based on variables such as age, gender, income, education level, marital status, and family size. These factors significantly influence consumer needs and purchasing behaviors.

2.2 Psychographic Segmentation

Psychographic segmentation considers consumers' psychological characteristics, such as personality, values, attitudes, interests, and lifestyles. This type of segmentation helps in understanding consumers' motivations and preferences more deeply.

2.3 Geographic Segmentation

Geographic segmentation divides the market based on geographic location, such as countries, regions, cities, or neighborhoods. Geographic differences can influence consumer preferences, purchasing behaviors, and specific needs.

2.4 Behavioral Segmentation

Behavioral segmentation is based on consumer behaviors, such as purchasing patterns, product usage, brand loyalty, and response to marketing campaigns. This type of segmentation allows identifying the most valuable consumers and developing strategies to retain them.

3. Creating Personas

Once the market is segmented, the next step is creating personas, which are fictional representations of ideal consumers based on the collected data. Personas help humanize the target audience and better understand their needs and preferences. Here's how to create effective personas:

3.1 Gathering Detailed Data

Collect detailed data on each market segment, including demographic, psychographic, geographic, and behavioral information. Use surveys, interviews, and data analysis to gain an in-depth understanding of consumers.

3.2 Identifying Common Patterns

Analyze the collected data to identify common patterns and group consumers based on similar characteristics. This allows creating representative personas of the main market segments.

3.3 Developing Persona Profiles

Create detailed profiles for each persona, including name, age, occupation, interests, goals, challenges, and purchasing behaviors. These profiles help visualize and better understand the target audience.

3.4 Using Personas in Branding Strategies

Use personas to guide all branding activities, from creating marketing messages to designing products and services. Personas help maintain a consumer focus and ensure all decisions are oriented toward satisfying their needs.

Examples of Market Analysis and Target Definition Methodologies

1. Surveys and Interviews

Surveys and interviews are effective tools for collecting primary data from consumers. These methods provide direct information on consumers' preferences, needs, and behaviors.

1.1 Surveys

Surveys can be distributed online, via email, or through market research platforms. Questions can be closed (with predefined answers) or open-ended (allowing detailed responses). Online surveys offer the advantage of reaching a wide audience and collecting data quickly and cost-effectively.

1.2 Interviews

Interviews can be conducted in person, over the phone, or via video conferencing. Interviews offer the opportunity to delve deeper into responses and gain qualitative insights. Semi-structured interviews, which combine predefined questions with open-ended questions, are particularly useful for exploring complex topics.

2. Focus Groups

Focus groups are guided discussion sessions with a group of consumers representative of the target audience. These groups allow exploring consumers' opinions, perceptions, and reactions interactively.

2.1 Preparing Focus Groups

Preparation includes selecting participants,

defining discussion questions, and choosing an experienced moderator. Creating a comfortable and unbiased environment is crucial to encourage active participation.

2.2 Conducting Focus Groups

During focus groups, the moderator guides the discussion, encouraging participants to share their opinions and experiences. It's essential to record the sessions for later analysis.

2.3 Analyzing Results

Analyzing focus group results involves identifying recurring themes and common opinions. These insights can inform branding strategies and improve understanding of the target audience.

3. Analysis of Secondary Data

Analyzing secondary data involves examining pre-existing data from external sources. These data can provide a general market overview and trends, supplementing primary data collected.

3.1 Sources of Secondary Data

Sources include market reports, industry studies, government statistics, research articles, and academic publications. These data can be found in libraries, online databases, government websites, and industry journals.

3.2 Advantages of Secondary Data Analysis

Secondary data analysis offers several advantages, including speed and reduced cost compared to primary data collection. Additionally, secondary data can provide a comparative basis for primary data and help validate conclusions.

3.3 Limitations of Secondary Data Analysis

However, secondary data analysis also presents some limitations. Data may not be specific to the company's needs and may be outdated. It's important to evaluate the quality and relevance of the data before using them.

Creating Branding Strategies Based on Market Analysis

Once market analysis is complete and the target audience defined, effective branding strategies can be developed. These strategies must align with the target audience's needs and preferences and leverage the company's strengths.

1. Brand Positioning

Brand positioning is the process of defining how the brand will be perceived by consumers relative to competitors. Clear and distinctive positioning helps differentiate the brand in the market and create a strong identity.

1.1 Defining Positioning

Defining positioning includes creating a unique value proposition and communicating the brand's distinctive benefits. It's important to consider the target audience's needs and preferences and the company's strengths.

1.2 Communicating Positioning

Positioning must be communicated through all consumer touchpoints, including visual branding, marketing messages, products, and services. Consistency is crucial to reinforce positioning in consumers' minds.

2. Creating Marketing Messages

Marketing messages must be personalized for the target audience and clearly communicate the brand's benefits. It's important to use language and style that resonate with the desired audience.

2.1 Developing Messages

Developing marketing messages includes creating slogans, headlines, copy, and content for various communication channels. Messages should be clear, compelling, and aligned with the brand's positioning.

2.2 Testing Messages

Before launching a marketing campaign, it's

useful to test messages with a representative sample of the target audience. This allows evaluating message effectiveness and making any necessary modifications before launch.

3. Choosing Communication Channels

Choosing communication channels depends on the habits and preferences of the target audience. It's important to select channels that allow reaching the desired audience effectively and cost-efficiently.

3.1 Traditional Channels

Traditional channels include television, radio, newspapers, magazines, and billboards. These channels can effectively reach a broad audience but can also be costly.

3.2 Digital Channels

Digital channels

include social media, websites, email, search engines, and online advertising. These channels offer several advantages, including targeted reach, real-time interaction, and the ability to measure results.

4. Evaluating and Adjusting Strategies

Finally, it's crucial to continuously evaluate the effectiveness of branding strategies and make necessary adjustments. This includes monitoring key performance indicators (KPIs), collecting consumer feedback, and staying updated on market trends.

4.1 Key Performance Indicators

KPIs may include brand awareness, market

share, customer satisfaction, sales, and return on investment. Monitoring these indicators helps evaluate the success of branding strategies and identify areas for improvement.

4.2 Consumer Feedback

Collecting consumer feedback through surveys, social media, and customer service interactions provides valuable insights into the brand's perception and areas for improvement.

4.3 Staying Updated

Staying updated on market trends, consumer preferences, and competitive strategies allows anticipating changes and adapting branding strategies accordingly.

Market analysis and target audience definition are crucial steps in creating an effective branding strategy. Thoroughly understanding the market and consumers allows developing personalized strategies that resonate with the target audience and create a strong brand identity. By following the methodologies and steps outlined in this document, companies can enhance their branding efforts and achieve long-term success.

4.Brand Identity, Brand Positioning Creation, and Brand Messaging Development

Building a strong brand is a complex process that requires strategic planning and meticulous execution. In this document, we will explore in detail three fundamental elements of branding: brand identity, brand positioning creation, and brand messaging development. These components are crucial for defining how a brand is perceived in the market, differentiating it from competitors, and effectively communicating with the target audience.

Brand Identity

1. Definition of Brand Identity

Brand identity is the set of visual, auditory, and sensory elements that represent a brand and distinguish it from others. It includes the brand name, logo, colors, fonts, tone of voice, and other elements that contribute to creating a coherent and recognizable image.

1.1 Elements of Brand Identity

- **Brand Name:** It must be memorable, easy to pronounce, and relevant to the target market.

- **Logo:** The logo is the visual symbol of the brand. It must be distinctive, simple, and versatile.

- **Colors:** The color palette should reflect the brand's personality and create a cohesive visual identity.

- **Fonts:** Fonts should be readable and consistent with the brand's style.

- **Tone of Voice:** The tone of voice should reflect the brand's personality and be used consistently across all communications.

- **Graphic Elements:** Icons, images, and patterns that support the brand's visual identity.

- **Packaging:** The design of the packaging contributes to the customer experience and should align with the brand identity.

2. Creation of Brand Identity

The creation of brand identity is a process that involves several stages, from initial research and analysis to the design and implementation of visual and communicative elements.

2.1 Research and Analysis

Initial research and analysis are fundamental to understanding the market, the target audience, and the competition. This step includes:

- **Market Analysis:** Understanding market trends, opportunities, and threats.

- **Competitor Analysis:** Examining major

competitors, their strengths and weaknesses, and their market positioning.

- **Target Audience Analysis:** Identifying the needs, desires, and behaviors of the target audience.

2.2 Brand Concept Development

The brand concept is the central idea that guides the creation of the brand identity. It includes:

- **Mission:** The brand's mission defines its purpose and long-term objectives.

- **Vision:** The vision describes how the brand sees the future and its role in the market.

- **Values:** The brand values represent the fundamental principles that guide all brand activities and decisions.

2.3 Design of Visual Elements

The next step is the design of visual elements, which includes:

- **Logo Design:** Creating a logo that effectively represents the brand identity.

- **Selection of Colors and Fonts:** Choosing a color palette and fonts that reflect the brand's personality.

- **Development of Graphic Elements and Packaging:** Creating graphic elements and packaging that are consistent with the brand's visual identity.

2.4 Creation of Tone of Voice

The tone of voice is how the brand communicates with the audience. It must be consistent with the brand's personality and adapted to the target audience.

2.5 Implementation and Consistency

Implementing the brand identity requires consistency across all activities and communication channels. This includes:

- **Marketing Materials:** Brochures, flyers, websites, social media, and other marketing materials should reflect the brand identity.

- **Internal Communication:** Ensuring that all employees understand and correctly use the brand identity.

- **Customer Experience:** The customer experience should align with the brand identity at all touchpoints.

Brand Positioning Creation

1. Definition of Brand Positioning

Brand positioning is the process of positioning the brand in the consumers' minds in a distinctive way relative to competitors. It is how the brand is perceived in the market and represents the brand's promise to consumers.

1.1 Objectives of Brand Positioning

- **Differentiation:** Differentiating the brand from competitors in a unique and relevant way.

- **Perceived Value:** Creating a positive and strong perceived value in consumers' minds.

- **Loyalty:** Building lasting relationships with consumers based on trust and satisfaction.

2. Process of Creating Brand Positioning

The process of creating brand positioning involves several stages, from understanding the market and target audience to defining the unique value proposition and communicating the positioning.

2.1 Understanding the Market and Target Audience

Understanding the market and target audience is fundamental for identifying positioning opportunities. This includes:

- **Market Segmentation:** Dividing the market into distinct segments based on demographic, psychographic, geographic, and behavioral characteristics.

- **Needs and Desires Analysis:** Identifying the needs, desires, and problems of the target audience.

2.2 Competitor Analysis

Competitor analysis helps identify the strengths and weaknesses of major competitors and discover differentiation opportunities.

- **Positioning Map:** Creating a positioning map to visualize how competitors position themselves in the market and identify gaps.

- **Differentiation Points Analysis:** Evaluating what makes the brand unique compared to competitors.

2.3 Defining the Unique Value Proposition

The unique value proposition (UVP) is the central element of brand positioning. It must be clear, relevant, and distinctive.

- **Functional Benefits:** What tangible benefits does the brand offer consumers?

- **Emotional Benefits:** What emotional

79

and psychological benefits does the brand offer?

- **Proof and Guarantees:** How can the brand demonstrate and guarantee the promised benefits?

2.4 Communicating Brand Positioning

Communicating brand positioning must be consistent across all touchpoints and clearly convey the unique value proposition.

- **Slogan and Tagline:** Creating a slogan or tagline that summarizes the brand's value proposition.

- **Marketing Messages:** Developing marketing messages that effectively communicate the brand's positioning.

- **Visual and Tone of Voice:** Ensuring that visual elements and tone of voice align with the brand's positioning.

3. Monitoring and Adjusting Brand Positioning

Monitoring and adjusting brand positioning are essential to maintaining relevance in an ever-evolving market.

- **Consumer Feedback:** Collecting feedback from consumers to evaluate how the brand is perceived.

- **Performance Analysis:** Monitoring performance metrics to evaluate the effectiveness of positioning.

- **Adaptation and Improvement:** Making adjustments and improvements to the brand positioning based on feedback and performance analysis.

Brand Messaging Development

1. Definition of Brand Messaging

Brand messaging is the set of key messages that a brand communicates to its audience. These messages must be consistent with the brand identity and positioning and resonate with the target audience.

1.1 Objectives of Brand Messaging

- **Clarity:** Clearly communicate the brand's value proposition and benefits.

- **Consistency:** Maintain consistency in messages across all communication channels.

- **Relevance:** Ensure messages are relevant to the target audience.

2. Process of Developing Brand Messaging

The process of developing brand messaging involves defining key messages, creating the tone of voice, and implementing messages across various communication channels.

2.1 Defining Key Messages

Key messages are the main ideas and information that the brand wants to communicate. They must be clear, compelling, and relevant to the target audience.

- **Value Proposition:** Communicate the brand's unique value proposition.

- **Product Benefits:** Highlight the functional and emotional benefits of the product.

- **Brand Values:** Communicate the fundamental values of the brand.

2.2 Creating the Tone of Voice

The tone of voice is how messages are communicated. It must reflect the brand's personality and resonate with the target audience.

- **Brand Personality:** Define the brand personality (e.g., friendly, professional, playful, serious) and ensure the tone of voice is consistent.

- **Channel Adaptation:** Adapt the tone of voice to different communication channels (e.g., formal for business emails, informal for social media).

2.3 Implementing Brand Messaging

Implementing brand messaging requires consistency across all communication channels and marketing materials.

- **Websites and Blogs:** Ensure the brand's website and blog reflect the key messages and tone of voice.

- **Social Media:** Use social media to consistently communicate the brand's messages and engage with the audience.

- **Advertising and Promotions:** Create advertising and promotional campaigns that communicate the brand's key messages.

- **Printed Marketing Materials:** Ensure brochures, flyers, and other printed materials reflect the brand's messages.

3. Monitoring and Optimizing Brand Messaging

Monitoring and optimizing brand messaging are essential to ensuring messages are effective and relevant.

- **Consumer Feedback:** Collect feedback from consumers to evaluate how messages are perceived.

- **Performance Analysis:** Monitor performance metrics to evaluate the effectiveness of messages.

- **Adaptation and Improvement:** Make adjustments and improvements to messages based on feedback and performance analysis.

Building a strong brand requires a deep understanding of brand identity, brand positioning, and brand messaging. Creating a distinctive brand identity, strategically positioning the brand in the market, and developing effective marketing messages are crucial elements for a brand's success. By following a structured and data-driven methodology, companies can create brands that resonate with their audience, build lasting relationships, and sustain a long-term competitive advantage.

5.Branding Tools: Launch, Logo and Visual Identity, Slogan and Storytelling, Integrated Communication, Digital Branding, and Brand Experience

In today's competitive landscape, effective branding is essential for any company's success. Branding isn't just about creating a catchy logo or name; it involves a complex, integrated strategy that includes various tools and techniques. This document will explore in detail the fundamental tools of branding, including launch, logo and visual identity, slogan and storytelling, integrated communication, digital branding, and brand experience. Each of these elements contributes to building and strengthening brand identity, creating emotional connections with the audience, and differentiating the brand from competitors.

Brand Launch

1. Launch Preparation

Launching a brand is a crucial moment that requires meticulous planning and a well-defined strategy. Launch preparation involves several stages, including market research, defining the target audience, developing the brand message, and creating a communication plan.

1.1 Market Research

Market research is essential to understand the context in which the brand will be launched. This includes analyzing market trends, identifying major competitors, and understanding the needs and expectations of the target audience.

1.2 Defining the Target Audience

Identifying the target audience is essential for developing a brand message that resonates with the desired audience. This process involves segmenting the market into distinct groups based on demographic, psychographic, and behavioral criteria.

1.3 Developing the Brand Message

The brand message must clearly communicate the unique value proposition and benefits of the brand. It must be compelling, relevant, and aligned with the needs and expectations of the target audience.

1.4 Creating a Communication Plan

The communication plan defines how, when, and where the brand will be presented to the public. This includes selecting communication channels, planning marketing campaigns, and defining launch activities.

2. Launch Strategy

An effective launch strategy must create brand awareness, generate interest, and stimulate action. This requires integrating various marketing and communication activities.

2.1 Pre-Launch

The pre-launch phase is crucial for creating anticipation and interest in the brand. This can include teasers, social media anticipation campaigns, exclusive events, and PR activities.

2.2 Launch

The launch phase is when the brand is officially presented to the public. This can include launch events, advertising campaigns, press releases, and digital marketing activities.

2.3 Post-Launch

The post-launch phase is important for maintaining interest and building long-term relationships with consumers. This can include follow-up activities, loyalty programs, regular updates, and continuous engagement on social media.

Logo and Visual Identity

1. Importance of Logo and Visual Identity

The logo and visual identity are fundamental elements of branding that help create a coherent and recognizable brand image. A well-designed logo and cohesive visual identity help differentiate the brand from competitors and create an emotional connection with the audience.

1.1 The Logo

The logo is the visual symbol of the brand and must be distinctive, simple, and versatile. It must reflect the essence of the brand and be easily recognizable in various contexts and sizes.

1.2 The Visual Identity

The visual identity includes all the visual elements that represent the brand, such as colors, fonts, images, icons, and patterns. It must be consistent and harmonious, and it must reflect the brand's personality.

2. Creating the Logo and Visual Identity

Creating the logo and visual identity requires a combination of creativity and strategy. The process involves several stages, from defining requirements to designing and implementing the visual elements.

2.1 Defining Requirements

Defining requirements is the first step in creating the logo and visual identity. This includes understanding the brand's mission, vision, and values, as well as the expectations of the target audience.

2.2 Designing the Logo

Designing the logo requires a combination of creativity and technical skills. The logo must be simple, memorable, and versatile. It must work well in black and white and at different sizes.

2.3 Developing the Visual Identity

The visual identity includes choosing colors,

fonts, and other visual elements that represent the brand. It must be consistent and reflect the brand's personality.

2.4 Implementation and Consistency

Implementing the visual identity requires consistency in all communication materials and touchpoints with the audience. This includes the website, marketing materials, packaging, and physical spaces.

Slogan and Storytelling

1. Importance of Slogan and Storytelling

The slogan and storytelling are powerful tools for communicating the brand's value proposition and creating an emotional connection with the audience. An effective slogan must be short, memorable, and reflect the brand's essence. Storytelling, on the other hand, allows the brand's story to be told in an engaging and authentic way.

1.1 The Slogan

A well-designed slogan must capture the essence of the brand in a few words. It must be easy to remember and pronounce, and it must resonate with the target audience.

1.2 Storytelling

Storytelling allows the brand's story to be told in an engaging and authentic way. It must be consistent with the brand's identity and reflect its values, mission, and vision.

2. Creating the Slogan and Storytelling

Creating the slogan and storytelling requires a combination of creativity and strategy. The process involves several stages, from defining key messages to creating content and implementing it.

2.1 Defining Key Messages

Defining key messages is the first step in creating the slogan and storytelling. This includes identifying the brand's unique benefits and its core values.

2.2 Creating the Slogan

Creating the slogan requires a combination of creativity and strategy. The slogan must be short, memorable, and relevant to the target audience.

2.3 Developing the Storytelling

Developing the storytelling involves creating

engaging content that tells the brand's story. This can include founder stories, case studies, customer testimonials, and other content that reflects the brand's identity.

2.4 Implementation and Consistency

Implementing the slogan and storytelling requires consistency in all communication materials and touchpoints with the audience. This includes the website, social media, marketing materials, and physical spaces.

Integrated Communication

1. Importance of Integrated Communication

Integrated communication is essential to ensure that all brand messages are consistent and coordinated across all communication channels. This helps build a strong and coherent brand image and avoid confusion and dissonance.

1.1 Message Consistency

Message consistency is fundamental to building a strong and coherent brand image. All messages must be aligned with the brand's identity and value proposition.

1.2 Channel Coordination

Coordinating communication channels is essential to ensure that messages are consistent and coordinated. This includes managing online and offline channels such as the website, social media, advertising, PR, and events.

2. Integrated Communication Strategies

Integrated communication strategies involve several stages, from planning to implementation and evaluation.

2.1 Communication Planning

Communication planning includes defining objectives, identifying the target audience, selecting communication channels, and creating a detailed communication plan.

2.2 Creating Messages

Creating messages requires consistency with the brand's identity and value proposition. Messages must be relevant to the target audience and adapted to different communication channels (radio, TV, web, industry journals and magazines).

2.3 Implementation and Coordination

Implementing and coordinating communication activities requires consistency across all channels and touchpoints with the audience. This includes the website, social media, advertising, PR, and events.

Digital Branding

Digital branding is the process of building and managing a brand's presence online. It involves using digital tools and platforms to create and maintain brand awareness, engagement, and loyalty.

1. Digital Presence

Creating a strong digital presence involves developing a user-friendly website, active social media profiles, and engaging content. This helps to reach and interact with the target audience online.

2. Online Reputation Management

Managing the brand's online reputation is crucial for maintaining a positive image. This includes monitoring and responding to customer reviews and feedback, as well as managing any negative publicity.

3. Digital Marketing

Digital marketing involves using various online channels such as search engines, social media, email, and content marketing to promote the brand. It helps to reach a wider audience and drive traffic to the brand's website.

Brand Experience

Brand experience encompasses all the

interactions a customer has with the brand, from initial awareness to post-purchase engagement. It is crucial for building brand loyalty and advocacy.

1. Customer Journey Mapping

Understanding the customer journey helps to identify key touchpoints and create a seamless and enjoyable brand experience. This involves mapping out all the steps a customer takes when interacting with the brand.

2. Customer Service

Providing excellent customer service is essential for creating a positive brand experience. This includes being responsive to customer inquiries and resolving any issues promptly.

3. Loyalty Programs

Implementing loyalty programs can help to reward repeat customers and encourage them to continue engaging with the brand. This can include discounts, exclusive offers, and special events for loyal customers.

By using these branding tools effectively, companies can build strong and memorable brands that resonate with their audience, create emotional connections, and stand out in the competitive market. Following a structured and data-driven approach, businesses can create brands that foster long-term relationships and sustain a competitive advantage.

6.Management and Monitoring of the Brand

Brand Equity, Brand Management, Measurement and Evaluation, Brand Auditing

Effective brand management is essential for ensuring the long-term success of a company in today's competitive market. Brand management involves not only the creation and positioning of the brand but also its continuous monitoring, performance evaluation, and the protection of its equity over time. This document will explore in detail the management and monitoring of the brand, the importance of brand equity, brand management strategies, brand measurement and evaluation, and the brand auditing process. Each of these aspects is crucial for ensuring the brand maintains its relevance, consistency, and value in the market.

Management and Monitoring of the Brand

1. Definition of Brand Management

Brand management is the process of overseeing and controlling the various activities that influence the perception and image of the brand among consumers and in the market in general. It includes strategic planning, implementation of branding activities, monitoring of brand performance, and crisis management.

1.1 Strategic Brand Planning

Strategic brand planning is the first step in effective brand management. This includes market analysis, setting brand objectives, identifying the target audience, and developing strategies to achieve these goals.

1.2 Implementation of Branding Activities

Implementing branding activities includes creating a consistent brand identity, positioning the brand in the market, developing effective marketing messages, and managing communication activities.

1.3 Monitoring Brand Performance

Monitoring brand performance involves the continuous evaluation of brand perception among consumers, measuring key branding metrics, and adjusting strategies based on the results.

1.4 Reputation Crisis Management

Reputation crisis management is crucial for protecting the brand's image in emergency or crisis situations. This includes crisis communication management, quick response to negative feedback, and repairing the brand's image.

Brand Equity

1. Importance of Brand Equity

Brand equity represents the commercial value and intangible capital associated with a brand. It is determined by consumer perceptions of product quality, brand trust, consumer loyalty, and positive associations with the brand.

1.1 Components of Brand Equity

- **Awareness:** The brand's recognition among consumers.

- **Perceived Quality:** Consumer perception of the quality of the product or service offered by the brand.

- **Brand Associations:** Positive or negative associations consumers link to the brand.

- **Brand Loyalty:** Consumer loyalty to the brand and their propensity to choose it over competitors.

- **Brand Assets:** The rights and marketing resources associated with the brand.

1.2 Benefits of Brand Equity

- **Trust and Credibility:** A brand with strong equity enjoys greater trust and credibility among consumers.

- **Premium Pricing:** Brands with high equity can justify premium prices for their products or services.

- **Crisis Resilience:** A brand with strong equity is more resilient during market or reputation crises.

- **Competitive Advantage:** Brand equity can create a sustainable competitive advantage in the long term.

Brand Management

1. Key Concepts in Brand Management

Brand management is the process of strategic management, development, and promotion of the brand to enhance its perception and value in the market. It includes various activities and strategies aimed at maintaining and strengthening the brand's identity and image.

1.1 Brand Consistency

Brand consistency is essential for maintaining a clear and recognizable perception of the brand among consumers. This includes consistency in marketing messages, visual design, and tone of voice.

1.2 Brand Innovation

Brand innovation involves introducing new

products, services, or initiatives that keep the brand relevant and competitive in the ever-evolving market.

1.3 Customer Relationship Management

Customer relationship management is crucial for creating an emotional connection with the audience and enhancing consumer loyalty. This includes personalizing customer experiences and effectively managing interactions.

1.4 Competitor Differentiation

Competitor differentiation is essential for uniquely and relevantly positioning the brand in the market. This can be achieved through innovation, effective communication, and creating unique value for consumers.

Brand Measurement and Evaluation

1. Importance of Brand Measurement

Brand measurement is essential for evaluating the effectiveness of branding strategies and identifying areas for improvement. This includes assessing branding metrics, market research, and consumer feedback.

1.1 Key Branding Metrics

- **Awareness:** The brand's recognition among consumers.

- **Perceived Quality:** Consumer perception of the quality of the product or service offered by the brand.

- **Brand Associations:** Positive or negative associations linked to the brand.

- **Brand Loyalty:** Consumer loyalty and their propensity to choose the brand over competitors.

1.2 Market Research

Market research is essential for gathering data and information on consumer behavior, market trends, and the brand's positioning relative to competitors.

1.3 Consumer Feedback

Consumer feedback provides direct information on brand perception and customer experiences. This can be collected through surveys, interviews, focus groups, and social media analysis.

2. Brand Evaluation

Brand evaluation involves analyzing the collected data to assess the effectiveness of branding strategies and identify areas for improvement.

2.1 Analysis of Strengths and Weaknesses

Analyzing the brand's strengths and weaknesses allows identifying areas where the brand excels and areas needing improvement.

2.2 Identification of Opportunities and Threats

Identifying market opportunities and threats helps guide future branding strategies and keeps the brand competitive.

2.3 Planning Corrective Actions

Based on the data analysis, corrective actions are planned to improve brand perception and strengthen its market positioning.

Brand Auditing

1. Definition of Brand Auditing

Brand auditing is the process of critically and analytically evaluating the brand's health and performance. This includes reviewing all aspects of the brand, from visual identity and messaging to consumer perception and customer relationship management.

1.1 Objectives of Brand Auditing

- **Evaluation of Brand Equity:** Measuring the commercial value and image of the brand in the market.

- **Identification of Improvement Opportunities:** Identifying areas where the brand can improve its competitive position.

- **Monitoring Brand Consistency:**

Ensuring all aspects of the brand are aligned with its identity and values.

- **Reputation Crisis Management:** Preventing and managing potential threats to the brand's reputation.

1.2 Brand Auditing Process

The brand auditing process includes several phases, from data collection to evaluating results and planning corrective actions.

- **Data Collection:** Gathering quantitative and qualitative data on consumer behavior, brand performance, and competition.

- **Data Analysis:** Analyzing the collected data to identify trends, strengths, and areas for brand improvement.

- **Performance Evaluation:** Assessing brand performance against strategic objectives and key branding metrics.

- **Planning Corrective Actions:** Based on

data analysis, planning corrective actions to improve brand perception and strengthen its market position.

Effective brand management requires a strategic and integrated approach that includes strategic planning, implementing branding activities, continuous monitoring of brand performance, and critical evaluation through brand auditing. Brand equity plays a crucial role in determining the brand's value and relevance in the market, while brand management ensures the brand maintains a consistent and positive presence among consumers. Measuring and evaluating the brand is essential for identifying improvement opportunities and addressing the challenges the brand may face in the competitive market. Finally, brand auditing provides a comprehensive view of the brand's health and guides strategic decisions to improve its performance and protect its reputation in the long term.

7. Implementation of Branding Strategy

Implementing an effective branding strategy requires a series of targeted and coordinated actions that contribute to building and strengthening the brand's identity in the market. Branding strategies are never one-size-fits-all and must be tailored to the specifics of the industry, target audience, and business objectives. In this document, we will explore 40 effective branding strategies, divided into key categories to facilitate a comprehensive and practical understanding.

1. Brand Identity Strategies

Brand identity strategies focus on clearly defining the essence of the brand and communicating it cohesively to the public.

1. **Defining Brand Mission, Vision, and Values:** Clearly articulate the brand's mission, vision, and core values to guide all

branding activities and communications.

2. **Creating Consistent Brand Identity:**
Develop a distinctive logo, colors, fonts, and
visual style that reflect the brand's identity and
values cohesively.

3. **Developing Brand Architecture:**
Define a clear hierarchical structure for sub-
brands and product lines, if applicable, to
facilitate cohesive brand management.

4. **Brand Personality:** Define a unique
personality for the brand that guides tone of
voice, communication style, and interactions
with the audience.

5. **Defining Unique Selling Proposition
(USP):** Identify and clearly communicate
what makes the brand unique and different
from the competition.

2. Brand Positioning Strategies

Brand positioning strategies aim to determine how the brand is perceived relative to competitors in the market.

6. **Competitive Analysis:** Conduct in-depth research on competitors to identify strengths, weaknesses, and effectively differentiate the brand.

7. **Market Segmentation:** Identify key market segments and tailor the brand's positioning strategy to maximize attractiveness for each segment.

8. **Market Targeting:** Clearly define the target audience based on demographic, psychographic, and behavioral characteristics.

9. **Developing Brand Positioning:** Define the desired brand positioning relative to

competitors (premium, value, convenience, etc.) and develop a strategy to achieve this positioning.

10. **Creating Positioning Messaging:** Develop clear and compelling messages that communicate the desired brand positioning to consumers.

3. Brand Communication Strategies

Brand communication strategies aim to build awareness, interest, and loyalty among consumers through consistent and engaging messaging.

11. **Planning Advertising Campaigns:** Develop creative and targeted advertising campaigns that reach the target audience through appropriate channels.

12. **Utilizing Social Media:** Leverage

social media to build a follower community, engage with customers, and effectively spread brand messages.

13. **Public Relations and Crisis Management:** Implement proactive PR strategies to manage the brand's image and respond promptly to reputation crises.

14. **Content Marketing:** Create informative, educational, or entertaining content that resonates with the audience and reinforces the brand's authority in its industry.

15. **Experiential Marketing:** Create memorable experiences for consumers through events, guerrilla marketing activities, or sponsorships that reflect the brand's values.

4. Customer Loyalty Strategies

Customer loyalty strategies aim to retain

existing customers and encourage repeat purchases and advocacy for the brand.

16. **Loyalty Programs:** Develop loyalty programs that reward loyal customers with incentives, discounts, or early access to new products.

17. **Customer Relationship Management (CRM):** Use CRM systems to manage customer interactions and personalize communications and offers based on individual preferences.

18. **Personalized Communications:** Send personalized messages, exclusive offers, and relevant content based on purchase behaviors and customer preferences.

19. **Customer Feedback:** Regularly gather feedback from customers through surveys, reviews, and interaction analysis to continuously improve the customer

experience.

20. **Proactive Customer Support:** Provide excellent customer service and promptly respond to customer questions, concerns, and issues.

5. Brand Innovation Strategies

Brand innovation strategies aim to maintain the brand's relevance in a continuously changing market.

21. **Developing New Products:** Introduce new products or services that meet emerging consumer needs or leverage new technologies.

22. **Collaborations and Partnerships:** Collaborate with other companies or influencers to expand the audience and access new markets.

23. **Continuous Research and Development:** Invest in research and development to constantly improve product quality, innovation, and sustainability.

24. **Adapting to Market Trends:** Monitor market trends and quickly adapt the brand strategy to stay ahead.

25. **Innovation in Marketing:** Use new marketing techniques and technologies, such as artificial intelligence or augmented reality, to engage the audience innovatively.

6. Brand Reputation Management Strategies

Brand reputation management strategies aim to protect and enhance the public image and perception of the brand.

26. **Online Reputation Monitoring:** Use monitoring tools to track brand mentions on social media, forums, and online reviews.

27. **Managing Customer Reviews:** Respond promptly to customer reviews, both positive and negative, to demonstrate support and customer care.

28. **Building Media Relations:** Develop positive relationships with journalists and influencers to gain favorable media coverage and increase brand visibility.

29. **Transparency and Authenticity:** Be transparent in communications and authentic in actions to earn consumer trust and improve brand reputation.

30. **Crisis Management:** Prepare crisis management plans to respond quickly and effectively to emergency situations that could damage the brand's reputation.

31. **Product Co-branding:** Launch collaborative products that combine the strengths and values of two distinct brands to create a more attractive offering for consumers.

32. **Co-marketing:** Develop joint marketing campaigns involving both brands to increase visibility and audience interest.

33. **Co-sponsoring Events:** Sponsor common events or initiatives that increase visibility and enhance the image of both brands.

34. **Collaboration for Social Causes:** Collaborate on corporate social responsibility (CSR) initiatives that reflect shared brand values and enhance both brands' reputations.

35. **Brand Licensing:** License the brand for use on products or services from other brands that meet the brand's standards of

quality and integrity.

8. Market Expansion Strategies

Market expansion strategies aim to penetrate new geographic or demographic markets to expand brand reach and growth.

36. **Internationalization of the Brand:** Adapt the branding strategy to successfully enter international markets, considering cultural differences and local preferences.

37. **Targeting New Market Segments:** Identify and target new market segments that offer growth and profitability opportunities for the brand.

38. **Adapting Marketing Strategy:** Customize the marketing strategy for each new market, using appropriate approaches and communication channels.

39. **Partnership with Local Distributors:**
Collaborate with local distributors or partners
who understand the local market and can
facilitate brand entry and growth.

40. **Risk and Opportunity Analysis:**
Conduct a detailed analysis of risks and
opportunities associated with brand expansion
to make informed and mitigated decisions.

Successfully implementing a branding
strategy requires an integrated and
multidimensional approach that includes
clearly defining the brand's identity, effective
market positioning, persuasive
communication, customer loyalty, continuous
innovation, proactive reputation management,
and exploring new market opportunities. The
40 strategies discussed in this document are
designed to provide a comprehensive
framework for the actions needed to build and
strengthen the brand in the long term,
dynamically adapting to changing market
conditions and consumer expectations.

Implementing these strategies requires ongoing commitment, adaptability, and a deep understanding of market dynamics and consumer behaviors.

Index